Rough Guides

25 Ultimate experiences

Mexico & Central America

Make the most of your time on Earth

ROUGH GUIDES

25 YEARS 1982–2007

NEW YORK • LONDON • DELHI

Contents

Introduction

EXPERIENCES have always been at the heart of the Rough Guide concept. A group of us began writing the books **25 years ago** (hence this celebratory mini series) and wanted to share the kind of travels we had been doing ourselves. It seems bizarre to recall that in the early 1980s, travel was very much a minority pursuit. Sure, there was a lot of tourism around, and that was reflected in the guidebooks in print, which traipsed around the established sights with scarcely a backward look at the local population and their life. We wanted to change all that: to put a country or a city's popular culture centre stage, to highlight the clubs where you could hear local music, drink with people you hadn't come on holiday with, watch the local football, join in with the festivals. And of course we wanted to push travel a bit further, inspire readers with the confidence and knowledge to break away from established routes, to find pleasure and excitement in remote islands, or desert routes, or mountain treks, or in street culture.

Twenty-five years on, that thinking seems pretty obvious: we all want to experience something real about a destination, and to seek out travel's **ultimate experiences**. Which is exactly where these **25 books** come in. They are not in any sense a new series of guidebooks. We're happy with the series that we already have in print. Instead, the **25s** are a collection of ideas, enthusiasms and inspirations: a selection of the very best things to see or do – and not just before you die, but now. Each selection is gold dust. That's the brief to our writers: there is no room here for the average, no space fillers. Pick any one of our selections and you will enrich your travelling life.

But first of all, take the time to browse. Grab a half dozen of these books and let the ideas percolate ... and then begin making your plans.

Mark Ellingham
Founder & Series Editor, Rough Guides

25

Ultimate
experiences
Mexico &
Central America

being serenaded by
MARIACHIS
in Guadalajara

Saturday night in downtown Guadalajara: the Plazuela de los Mariachis, squeezed into a corner of the colonial heart of the city, reverberates with the sounds of instruments being tuned. You'll no doubt recognize the violins, trumpets and guitars; more exotic to the ear – and unique to the music you're about to hear – are the vihuela, a small plinky guitar with a bowed back, and the guitarron, a large bass guitar. For time-honoured tunes, you're in the right spot: Guadalajara, the most traditional of Mexico's cities, is also the birthplace of mariachi, the country's famous musical export.

A smartly dressed couple – he with hair slicked back and she in her best dress – starts the festivities with a request for an old love song. The mariachis line up around their table, forming a wall of *charro* (nineteenth-century cowboy) outfits: large bow ties, gleaming belt buckles, jackets and trousers decorated with embroidery and silver fastenings. A trumpeter raises his instrument to

Guadalajara is 350km northwest of Mexico City (buses every 15min; 7–9hr). There are direct flights from several US cities, including Houston, Los Angeles and San Francisco. Every September the city hosts performers from all over the world for the **Festival de los Mariachis** (Ⓦwww .mariachi-jalisco.com.mx), ten days of concerts, parades and outdoor events.

his lips, and the first familiar notes of *Cielito Lindo* ("Ay, ay, ay, ay, canta y no llores") float over the square. Another song follows, then another. The couple gets to their feet and begins to waltz slowly between the packed café tables. Several troupes join the fray, serenading elderly couples, students, young lovers, fascinated travellers. Each group competes to be louder and more flamboyant than the next, and the noise – a melodious cacophony – is ear-splitting. As empty beer bottles and shot glasses pile up, all the Mexicans present start to sing along; there is not a word left out, not a beat missed.

Fittingly, the evening winds down with several howled rounds of one of the most popular mariachi tunes: "Guadalajara, Guadalajara, tienes el alma de provinciana, hueles a limpia rosa temprana" ("you have the soul of the provinces, you smell of fresh early roses").

02 Turtle-watching in Tortuguero

It's a clear, moonless night when we assemble for our pilgrimage to the beach. I can't understand how we are going to see anything in the blackness, but the guide's eyes seem to penetrate even the darkest shadows. We begin walking, our vision adjusting slowly.

We've come to Tortuguero National Park, in northeast Costa Rica, to witness sea turtles nesting. Once the domain of only biologists and locals, turtle-watching is now one of the more popular activities in ecotourism-friendly Costa Rica. As the most important nesting site in the western Caribbean, Tortuguero sees more than its share of visitors – since 1980, the annual number of observers has gone from 240 to 50,000.

The guide stops, points out two deep furrows in the sand – the sign of a turtle's presence – and places a finger to his lips, making the "shhh" gesture. The nesting females can be spooked by the slightest noise or light. He gathers us around a crater in the beach; inside it is an enormous creature. We hear her rasp and sigh as she brushes aside sand for her nest.

In whispers, we comment on her plight: the solitude of her task, the low survival rate of her hatchlings – only one of every 5000 will make it past the birds, crabs, sharks, seaweed and human pollution to adulthood.

We are all mesmerized by the turtle's bulk. Though we are not allowed to get too close, we can catch the glint of her eyes. She doesn't seem to register our presence at all. The whirring sound of discharged sand continues. After a bit the guide moves us away. My eyes have adapted to the darkness now, and I can make out other gigantic oblong forms labouring slowly up the beach – a silent, purposeful armada.

need to know

Tortuguero is 3–4hr north of Limón by boat. Several tour operators in San José and Limón offer tour packages to Tortuguero. Independent travellers must buy tickets for **Tortuguero National Park** from the information kiosk in the village (5–6pm; 3608c) and arrange for a certified tour guide (5154c). Tours leave nightly at 8pm and 10pm.

03 *roaming the*
ZAPATISTA HEARTLAND:
traditional villages near San Cristóbal

As the chanting reached a crescendo and the incense thickened to a fog, the chicken's neck snapped like a pencil. The seemingly ageless executioner sat on a carpet of pine needles, surrounded by hundreds of candles, his eyes fixed upon a brightly painted saintly icon. The man took a swig from a Coca-Cola bottle, a sign not of globalization, but of the expurgating power of soda – the Tzotzil people believe that evil spirits can be expulsed through a robust burp. Here, inside the church of San Juan de Chamula, such faith doesn't seem all that far-fetched.

This is the Zapatista heartland of Chiapas, a lost world of dense jungle and indigenous villages where descendants of the Maya cling to the rituals of their ancestors. Throughout the region, the iconography of Subcomandante Marcos, guerilla leader and poster child of the struggle for indigenous rights, reveals a continuing undercurrent of rebellion – San Cristóbal de las Casas, one of Mexico's most alluring towns, was the site of an armed Zapatista revolt in 1994.

Zincantán (10km from San Cristóbal) and **San Juan Chamula** (12km from San Cristóbal) are easily reached by bus. A permit (M$11) is required from the tourist office in town to enter the church of San Juan Chamula. Due to continuing low-intensity guerilla warfare, check the political situation before visiting the villages. Dedicated to the study, education and protection of the indigenous peoples, **Na-Bolom**, in the center of San Cristóbal, is an invaluable stop before exploring.

Outside San Cristóbal, the village of Chamula is literally a law unto itself, with its own judges, jail and council. Timeless rituals are revealed: women sell brightly coloured, hand-woven garments in the main square, returning home at midday to prepare a meal for their husbands, many of whom are shared (men can have up to three wives at a time). Every year during the pre-Lenten festival, perhaps the most exciting time to visit, the village's men run barefoot through blazing wheat.

Four kilometres from Chamula, Zincantán is equally fascinating. Here, the men, in red-and-white ponchos and flat hats strewn with ribbons (tied if they are married, loose if not), launch rockets skyward to stir the gods into sending rain. The women pummel tortillas and weave textiles, always with a watchful eye on the sky – many houses have gone up in smoke as a result of rogue fireworks.

04 *all aboard the*
COPPER CANYON RAILWAY

As the countryside – by turns savage, pristine, lush – flashes past the windows of the Chihuahua-Pacific Express, Mexico reveals a side of itself that is both spectacular and unexpected.

"El Chepe", as the train is known, traverses the country's most remote landscape, a region of rugged splendour called the Copper Canyon.

Spanning six prodigious canyons and a labyrinth of some two hundred gorges, this natural wonder is four times the size of the Grand Canyon. Harsh, inaccessible and thoroughly untamed, the canyons are sparsely populated only by the Rarámuri, an indigenous agrarian people.

El Chepe's journey commences on Mexico's Pacific coast, in Los Mochis, then trundles through 75km of arid, cactus-strewn wasteland to placid El Fuerte, the gateway to the canyons. From here, the track climbs, the air cools and the scenery shifts: for the next six hours, you roll past one incredible vista after another. In a continual skyward ascent, El Chepe plunges in and out of tunnels, rattles over bridges and makes hair-pin turns.

Colossal stone cliffs, folds of rock and serpentine rivers flicker by. Above you, mountains rise like fortified cities, while gaping chasms open on either side. Then, all at once, the stone corridor yields to a sweeping plateau of pine-scattered towers and stratified monoliths.

At Divisadero, 300km from Los Mochis and 2000m above sea level, three canyons converge to form an astonishing panorama. The train makes a brief stop here, giving you time to snap some pictures and breathe in the ozone and pine. Creel, another 60km along, is the place to stop for extended excursions – forests, gorges, waterfalls and hot springs all lie within easy reach.

The 655km expedition concludes on the desert plains of Chihuahua, though it feels as if you've travelled further. Stepping off the train, you're as likely to feel humbled as you are exhilarated.

CHIHUAHUA

CUACHTEMOC

CREEL · SAN JUANITO

BARRANCAS · DIVISIDERO

TEMORIS

BAHUICHIVO

EL FUERTE

LOS MOCHIS

It's not surprising that the beach in La Libertad is packed on Sundays. The port town is less than an hour's drive from the choked capital of El Salvador, its oceanfront restaurants serve the finest *mariscada* (creamy seafood soup) in the country and, of course, there's *el surf*.

The western end of the beach has one of the longest right point breaks, prosaically called *punta roca* (rocky point), in the world. On a good day – and with year-round warm water and consistent and uncrowded waves there are plenty of those – skilled *surfistas* can ride a thousand yards from the head of the point into the beach. Amateur surfers, meanwhile, opt for the section of gentler waves, known as *La Paz*, that roll into the mid-shore.

It's rare to walk through the town without seeing one of the local boys running barefoot, board under arm, down to the sea or hanging outside the Hospital de las Tablas while a dent or tear is repaired. Some, like Jimmy Rottingham, whose American father kick-started the ex-pat surf scene when he arrived in the 1970s (witness the psychedelic surfboards on the walls of *Punta Roca* restaurant), have become semi-professional.

If you're looking for quieter, cleaner breaks, join the foreign surfers who head west of La Libertad to beaches like El Zonte. These days it's a backpacker heaven, but until 1998 the point break here was secret among locals and students from Santa Tecla. The village's best surfer, El Teco, was inspired to jump on a board after watching *Hawaii Five-O*, later polishing his technique by observing pelicans surfing the waves. Even if you miss out on *olas de mantequilla* (waves like butter) or suffer too many *wipeadas* there's always the Zonte scene: at weekends the capital's hip kids come down to party amid bonfires, fire dancers and all-night drumming.

Surfing
near
La Libertad

need to know

Puerto La Libertad (often reduced to "El Puerto" by bus drivers) is 34km south of San Salvador; there are frequent buses (#102; 45min). There are also buses from the international airport. In **La Libertad** you can rent boards from **Mango's Lounge surf shop** and **Punta Roca**. **Hotel Horizonte Surf Resort** rents boards in **El Zonte**; prices are approximately M$110 per day. You'll find half a dozen accommodations in La Libertad – several are dirt cheap and none very special. The surfing villages along the coast all have decent places to stay.

Baja California

The *taco de pescado* – Baja California's gift to locals, dust-caked off-road explorers and cruise-boat day-trippers alike – exemplifies the simple pleasures that make the peninsula so appealing.

Constructed by piling freshly fried pieces of white fish on two warm corn tortillas and topping with shredded cabbage, a little light mayo, a splash of hot sauce and a squirt of lime, the *taco de pescado* is Mexican food at its most basic and delicious. Like all great street food, fish tacos taste better when served somewhere devoid of any atmosphere – most choice locations lack a proper floor, ceiling, walls or any combination thereof. The quality of the tacos corresponds directly to the length of time it takes for the cook to get them to you, then for you to get them into your mouth.

Ensenada, a large fishing center on the peninsula's northwest coast, is one of the best places to sample the *taco de pescado* – it's said that the dish was first concocted here by Japanese fishermen. Fifteen minutes inland from the port and the Mercado Negro fish market lies a well-established street vendor, **Tacos Fenix**. The three-person outfit operates from the sidewalk: one person preps the ingredients, a second mans the frying pan and the third handles the money and drinks. You don't have to know much Spanish (beyond *por favor* and *gracias*) to order; just listen and watch the people in front of you. And don't worry about the juices running down your hand after the first bite – getting dirty is part of the fun.

need to know
There are hourly bus services to **Ensenada** from Tijuana (1hr 30min). **Tacos Fenix** is on Calle Espinosa, at Calle Juárez; fish tacos go for under M$10. If you're on the Sea of Cortez side of Baja, you'll find plenty of good places to go for tacos along the coast in San Felipe, Bahía de los Ángeles, Loreto and La Paz.

The dense jungles of northern Guatemala, once the heartland of the Maya civilization, were home to dozens of thriving cities during Classic Maya times (250–909 AD). Tikal was arguably the greatest of them all, controlling an empire of vassal states and trade routes between the southern highlands and the Caribbean. The symbols of its dominance – six great temples – still stand.

Impressive at any time of day, Tikal shows itself to full advantage in the hours around sunrise. Because of the nature of the terrain – the extreme humidity of the forest usually shrouds the sun's early rays – it's rare to actually see the sun come up over the jungle. But even without a perfect sunrise, as the ruins of this Maya city come to life around you, dawn is still a magical time.

As day breaks, head for the top of Temple IV or Temple V. An ocean of green unfurls before you, the jungle canopy broken only by the chalk-white roofcombs of the other pyramids, soaring over the giant ceiba and zapote trees. The forest's denizens gradually begin to appear, emerging from their night-time resting places. Flocks of green parakeets career over the temple tops and keel-billed toucans hop along bromeliad-rich branches. Howler monkeys are at their most vociferous at dawn, their roars echoing around the graceful plazas and towering temples. Many of the animals that live in Tikal have become accustomed to seeing humans, so you're virtually guaranteed to come across packs of playful racoon-like coati snuffling through the undergrowth or the startling blue-chested ocellated turkey strutting around in search of its first feed of the day. As the sun climbs higher in the sky and the heat of the day increases, things begin to calm down. By 9am, when the large tour groups roll in, nature's activity has all but faded away, until the jungle awakes the next morning.

need to know

Entrance to **Tikal National Park** (daily 6am–6pm) is Q60. There are three hotels in the park, the best value of which is the **Jungle Lodge** (Ⓦwww.junglelodge.guate.com). **El Remate** (32km) and **Flores** (66km) also have plentiful accommodation. Minibuses (5am–6pm, Q40 return) run from both towns to Tikal every thirty minutes or so.

07

dawn at
TIKAL

The view from the boat is beautiful, with the variegated blues and greens of the Caribbean stretching toward the Yucatán coast on one side, and palm trees bowing over Cozumel's pearly white beach on the other.

From the surface, though, you'd never know that the most stunning sight of all is directly beneath you: Palancar Reef, a 5km stretch of some of the globe's richest coral beds, and the kind of vivid world people tend to imagine only with the aid of hallucinogens. Teeming with marine life, Palancar is just one small part of the Mesoamerican Barrier Reef, which stretches from Mexico to Honduras, but it is in a prime position to flourish. Just off the southwest corner of the island of Cozumel, and part of a larger ring of coral around much of the island, it is washed by slow, steady currents that keep the water clear and bear nutrients from nearby mangrove swamps.

Bumped by clumsy snorkellers, battered by hurricanes and boiled by freakish spikes in water temperature, Palancar not only survives but prospers as a fascinating and complex ecosystem. Any diver, novice or expert, could explore this reef for hours – or, if you're Jacques Cousteau, who put this place on divers' maps in the 1960s, years. Lobsters pick their way delicately along outcrops, feelers blown by the current, while blue-green parrotfish gnaw at the coral with their beaky mouths. (Their digestive system produces the powdery sand that slopes away into the deep-blue distance.) Striped clownfish hide in the protective tentacles of an anemone, immune to its toxic sting; mellow turtles graze on algae; a graceful ray glides by. All this happens as if in a dream, in near-complete silence – the only audible sound is the rush of your own breath.

Lovely as the surface world is, when you come up for air, it will all seem impossibly drab.

08 diving at Palancar Reef

Lovely as the surface world is, when you come up for air, it will all seem impossibly drab

need to know

All visitors to **Palancar Reef** must pay a national marine park fee of M$20, usually included in the tour rate. **Cozumel** has scores of dive operators; **Deep Blue** (℡987/872-5653, ⊛www.deepbluecozumel.com) is recommended. Two-tank dives cost about M$700; three-hour snorkelling trips are M$450.

09 *Encountering* Kuna culture

It's often said that there's an island for every day of the year in the San Blas archipelago. In fact, there are slightly more than that in this chain of coral atolls that stretches for 375km along the Caribbean coast of Panama. This is Kuna Yala, the autonomous homeland of the Kuna Indians, one of the most independent indigenous cultures in Central America. Even if you haven't heard of the Kuna before, you've probably seen them: the women, wearing piratical headscarves, gold nose rings and colourful traditional costumes are the pin-ups of the indigenous world. With palm-fringed beaches and coral reefs, Kuna Yala is the stuff of Caribbean dreams, but it is the Kuna themselves, with their rich cultural traditions, that most people come here to see.

In some ways, visiting Kuna Yala gives a feel of what the Caribbean must have been like before European colonists arrived. No outside development is allowed – non-Kuna cannot own land or property. You'll need to ask permission of a community's headman, or *sahila*, if you wish to visit a particular town or island, and you must be accompanied by a Kuna guide. Around forty of the islands are inhabited; some are home to several thousand people, while others are narrow sandbanks sheltering only a few families.

Despite the regulations, you can still explore Kuna culture and your natural surroundings pretty widely. Travelling by motorized dug-out canoe, your guide will take you to pristine beaches and reefs where you can swim and snorkel, as well as to other island communities. You may even be lucky enough to witness a traditional religious ceremony or join a fiesta in a communal hall (*casa de congreso*), where poet-historians sing myths and legends from hammocks, leaving you with a lasting impression of the Kuna heritage.

need to know

Regular daily flights leave Panama City to several different islands in **Kuna Yala**. You can also reach Kuna Yala on foot, through the rainforest from the **Nusagandi Nature Reserve** on the mainland. For any long stay, you must get permission from the Congreso General Kuna in Panama City (☎316 1233). A number of larger islands provide accommodation; the **Hotel San Blas** (☎290 6528) on Nalunega is an enduring favourite.

The colourful boats shunt their way out along the canals, provoking lots of good-natured shouting from the men wielding the poles

need to know
Xochimilco lies 28km southeast of Mexico City. Take the Metro to **Tasqueña station** (line 2), and from there the **Tren Ligero** to Xochimilco. The *embarcaderos* are well signposted from the station. There are also buses to Xochimilco from the centre of **Mexico City,** with extra services on Sundays. Prices for boat rides vary, but are usually M$132–154 per person per hour, plus the cost of any extras you purchase while onboard.

10 *floating through* XOCHIMILCO

S pend a few days in the intoxicating, maddening *centro histórico* of Mexico City, and you'll understand why thousands of Mexicans make the journey each Sunday to the "floating gardens" of Xochimilco, the country's very own Venice.

Built by the Aztecs to grow food, this network of meandering waterways and man-made islands, or *chinampas*, is an important gardening centre for the city, and where families living in and around the capital come to spend their day of rest. Many start their trip with a visit to the beautiful sixteenth-century church of San Bernadino in the suburb's main plaza, lighting candles and giving thanks for the day's outing. Duty done, they head down to one of several docks, or *embarcaderos*, on the water to hire out a *trajinera* for a few hours. These flat, brightly painted gondolas – with names like *Viva Lupita, Adios Miriam, El Truinfo, Titanic* – come fitted with table and chairs, perfect for a picnic.

The colourful boats shunt their way out along the canals, provoking lots of good-natured shouting from the men wielding the poles. As the silky green waters, overhung with trees, wind past flower-filled meadows, the cacophony and congestion of the city are forgotten. Mothers and grannies unwrap copious parcels and pots of food, men open bottles of beer and aged tequila; someone starts to sing. By midday, Xochimilco is full of carefree holiday-makers.

Don't worry if you haven't come with provisions – the *trajineras* are routinely hunted down by vendors selling snacks, drinks and even lavish meals from small wooden canoes. Others flog trinkets, sweets and souvenirs. And if you've left your guitar at home, no problem: boatloads of musicians – mariachis in full costume, marimba bands and wailing *ranchera* singers – will cruise alongside or climb aboard and knock out as many tunes as you've money to pay for.

The island of Utila, off the coast of Honduras, isn't your ordinary scuba-diving base. Sure, there's plenty of stunningly beautiful marine life to be seen. It isn't the beautiful, though, that draws many diving enthusiasts here. Rather, it's the exotically monstrous – Utila is one of the few places on Earth that the whale shark, the world's largest fish, can be spotted year-round.

Whale sharks, which are harmless to humans, remain elusive creatures – relatively little is known about them, and their scientific name (*rhincodon typhus*) wasn't even established until 1984. Measuring up to an estimated fifteen metres (and twenty tonnes), they are filter feeders, sieving tropical seas for nutrients and migrating across oceans and up and down the coast of Central America. Oceanic upswells close to Utila consistently sweep together a rich soup of plankton and krill, making them a prime feeding ground for the immense creatures.

Most mornings, dive boats scour the seas north of Utila between reef dives looking for "boils": feeding frenzies created by bonito tuna rounding up huge schools of baitfish, or krill. Hungry sharks home in on the boils, gliding just below the surface, mouths agape as they scythe through the sea. Their blue-grey upper bodies are sprinkled with intricate patterns of white spots (which appear electric blue from a distance in the sunlight), interspersed with checkerboard-style markings.

Often, they feed upright, an astonishing sight – watch as the great fish manoeuvre themselves into a vertical position, bobbing up and down and gulping seawater into two-metre-wide mouths. If you'd like, slip into the water with them. But do it while you can – the chance to swim among them is usually fleeting, as the boils disintegrate rapidly and the sharks disappear as quickly as they came.

11 CHASING WHALE SHARKS
NEAR UTILA

need to know

Utila has several daily flights (25min) and a daily ferry connection with **La Ceiba** on the mainland. Snorkelling and dive boat trips cost around L$283 per person, including all gear; **Utila Dive Center** (@www.utiladivecenter.com) is highly recommended. There is plenty of budget accommodation on the island.

12 Market day in Oaxaca

Oaxaca is pure magical realism – an elegant fusion of colonial grandeur and indigenous mysticism. From the zócalo, the city's main square, streets unfold in a patchwork of belle époque theatres, romantic courtyards and sublime churches.

need to know
Oaxaca is southeast of Mexico City, and can be reached by both bus (6–7hr) and plane (several flights daily). Saturday is market day. **Mercado de Abastos**, also known as Central de Abastos, is near the second-class bus station on Periférico, three blocks south of Independencia. Beware of pickpockets; they are active in all the main markets and squares.

While the city's colonial history reaches its zenith in the breathtaking Iglesia de Santo Domingo, pre-Hispanic traditions ignite in its kaleidoscopic markets.

The largest of these is the bustling Mercado de Abastos, which bombards the senses with riotous colours, intoxicating aromas and exotic tastes.

Indigenous women dressed in embroidered *huipiles,* or tunics, squat amidst baskets overflowing with red chillis and *chapulines* (baked grasshoppers), weaving *pozahuancos,* wrap-around skirts dyed with secretions from snails. Stalls are piled with *artesanía* from across the region. Leather sandals, or *huaraches,* are the specialty of Tlacolula; made from recycled tires, they guarantee even the most intrepid backpacker a lifetime of mileage.

Hand-woven rugs from Teotitlán del Valle, coloured using century-old recipes including pomegranate and cochineal beetles, are the most prized. The shiny black finish on the pottery from San Bartolo Coyotepec gives it an ornamental function – a promotion from the days when it was used to carry *mescal* to market.

Street-smart vendors meander the labyrinth alleyways, offering up the panaceas of ancient deities – *tejate*, the "Drink of the Gods", is a cacao-based beverage with a curd consistency and muddy hue. (A more guaranteed elixir is a mug of hot chocolate, laced with cinnamon and chilli, from *Mayordormo*, the Willy Wonka of Oaxaca.) The stalls around the outer edges of the market sell shots of mescal; distilled from the sugary heart of the cactus-like maguey plant and mixed with local herbs, it promises a cure to all ailments. With a dead worm at the bottom as proof of authenticity, it's an appropriately mind-bending libation for watching civilization and supernaturalism merge on a grand scale.

13

A glimpse of the murals
at Bonampak

For almost a century, scholars studying ancient Maya culture believed the Maya to be pacifists, devoted to their arcane calendar and other harmless pursuits. It wasn't until 1946, when a few Lacandón Maya led an American photographer to a ruined temple at Bonampak, deep in the Chiapas jungle, that they had any reason to think differently.

As the party entered the narrow building perched at the top of the temple and torchlight played across its interior, the ancient Maya flickered into living colour. A series of murals covered the walls and ceilings of three rooms, depicting the Maya in fascinating detail. Lords paraded in yellow-spotted jaguar pelts and elaborate headdresses, while attendants sported blue-green jade jewelry.

More remarkable was the quantity of bright-red gore splashed on scenes throughout the rooms: severed heads rolled, prisoners oozed blood from mangled fingers, sacrifice victims littered the ground. On one wall, eighth-century king Chan Muan glowered mercilessly at writhing captives, while on another his soldiers engaged in a frenzied battle.

The artistry of the murals was undeniable: even the most gruesome images – like the king's wife threading a thorn-studded rope through her tongue – were balanced by lush colours and captivating precision. But the discovery, while offering unparalleled insight for anthropologists and Maya experts, must have been somewhat unsettling too: to see Chan Muan poised to lop the head off a prisoner was astounding.

Visiting the Bonampak murals is slightly easier now than it was when they were found sixty years ago, but only just. They remain buried far enough in the humid Lacandón forest that you can still feel – when you step into the dimly lit rooms – a sense of drama and revelation.

14 riding down the Río San Juan

It was the end of a hot day in earthquake-flattened Managua. "There," I hissed in frustration, pointing at a poster on the wall, "that is where I want to go".

I had seen the photograph before, slapped up on café, bar and shop walls all over Nicaragua. The prize-winning photo, chosen by the tourist board to promote the country's pristine beauty, does not show the colonial streets of Granada. Nor does it illustrate the volcanoes of Ometepe or the cayes off the Caribbean coast.

Instead, it depicts a bend in a wide blue river, fringed by green meadows and dotted with small boats. The waterway is the 170-kilometre-long Río San Juan, which starts at vast Lake Nicaragua, runs along the country's border with Costa Rica and finally spills into the Caribbean Sea.

need to know

Four boats a day leave **San Carlos** for
El Castillo (2hr 30min; last boat back 2pm).
Two boats a week (Tues and Fri 5am; 10hr) travel
the whole length of the river to the Caribbean Sea.
There are several accommodation options in El Castillo.

The river has a rich – if tumultuous – history: it once carried supplies from Spain to its new colony and was besieged by pirates who came to sack Granada. Now better known for its ecotourism opportunities, the Río San Juan is surrounded by some of the most peaceful wilderness in Central America. Hundreds of species of wildlife live along its banks, from caimans, herons, manatees and jaguars to howler monkeys, sloths and flocks of rainbow-coloured parrots – don't forget your camera.

Remote as the river is, carved into dense rainforest, there is one notable pocket of civilization. In contrast to the small collection of ramshackle fishing villages along its banks, and sleazy San Carlos at its head, the old Spanish fort of El Castillo, two and a half hours downstream, shimmers like a mirage. Its waterfront is lined with wooden homes on stilts, their porches covered in carefully tended plants and connected by a meandering lane. The lovely setting is framed with a ruined castle atop a grassy knoll. And at the end of the village, as it seeps gently back into the forest, is the bend in the river in the photograph.

15
a taste of
mole poblano
in Puebla

Visitors to Mexico may find some of the country's culinary offerings a bit odd – not only do fried grasshoppers, baked maggots and raw ant eggs occasionally appear, but the national dish, mole poblano, combines two flavours, chilli and chocolate, that would seem to have little use for each other. Mole (or mólli), a Nahuatl word, means "mixture", of which there are actually dozens in Mexico; mole poblano, the most revered, comes from Puebla.

A rich sauce normally served with turkey or chicken, *mole poblano* can boast upwards of thirty ingredients; the most cherished recipes are guarded like state secrets. Fruits, nuts and spices are toasted over a fire, ground by hand and mixed into a paste. The chocolate, added at the last minute, is in its traditional unsweetened form, powdered cacao seeds.

The dish was created in the seventeenth century in the kitchens of the Convento de Santa Rosa for a banquet. It's still made for special occasions: no wedding in Puebla is complete without the women spending days preparing their *mole poblano* in huge black cauldrons. Among Cholulteca families, a live turkey is considered the guest of honour at wedding receptions; the bird is slaughtered the next day to serve as the base for the newlyweds' first *mole*.

A prime time to sample the sauce is during the Festival of Mole Poblano, held on three consecutive Sundays each July, when local restaurants compete to have their *mole* judged the city's best. The dish also stars on menus across the city on the fifth of May, or Cinco de Mayo, a national holiday that celebrates the defeat of Napoleon's invading army in Puebla in 1872. After the festivities, join the crowds and top off the night by feasting on the city's savoury speciality.

need to know

Puebla lies 100km southeast of Mexico City and is served by frequent buses (2hr). The city's best restaurants are clustered around the zócalo and the Plazuela de los Sapos. Recommended are **La Guadalupana**, 5 Oriente 605, Plazuela de los Sapos, and **Mesón Sacristía de la Compañia**, 6 Sur 304. You can buy *mole* paste (M$33 for a small jar) at the **Mercado 5 de Mayo,** north of the zócalo between 16 and 18 Poniente.

16 observing
Semana Santa
in Antigua

Combining solemn Catholic ritual and a distinctly Latin American passion for colour and clamour, the Easter week processions in Antigua, Guatemala, are a spectacular affair. By far the largest such processions in the western hemisphere, the annual event involves virtually the entire population of the city and its surrounding villages, and draws in tens of thousands of visitors from all over the globe.

Preparations begin far in advance, with residents spending hours creating dazzling *alfombras* (carpets) using coloured sawdust, flower petals and pine needles; the intricate displays often cover several blocks of the city's streets. Then, beginning the weekend before Easter, colossal wooden floats known as *andas* (some weigh over three tonnes), each topped with an image of Christ or another biblical figure, are carried through the streets. Step-by-step, the bearers shuffle towards the city's churches, their labourious progress grinding the meticulously assembled carpets into the dirt. Accompanying the processions are trumpeters playing funeral elegies, while clouds of thick copal incense hang over the streets. Many Antigueños wear period costume for the processions, albeit with a slightly modern flare: look closely and you'll see that the Roman centurions' helmet plumes are actually upended broom heads, and the Arabs are wearing Nike sports shoes beneath their purple robes.

The processions gain in intensity and fervour throughout the week, with Good Friday witnessing the most dramatic events. Starting at 3am, as Christ's death sentence is announced and the symbolic search for him begins, the cobbled lanes reverberate with the pounding of horses' hooves – the Roman cavalry. Massive, intricate *andas* emerge from the city's main churches later in the morning, toiling along carpet after carpet, while smaller ones, bourn by women with statues of the Virgin Mary, follow close behind. Events culminate two days later, on Easter Sunday, as Christ comes forward from the church of San Pedro to shouts of "Que viva el Rey" ("Long live the King").

need to know

Antigua is 45km west of Guatemala City, and is served by regular buses (every 15min; 1hr). Reserve hotel rooms for Semana Santa months in advance, and double-check your reservation as the week approaches. The **tourist office** in Antigua (☎832 0763) has listings of the week's events and maps showing the routes of the processions.

17 taking a dip
in the Yucatán's
cenotes

*Nature's perfect
swimming spots,
cenotes are filled with
cool fresh water year-round*

The Yucatán Peninsula can be unpleasantly muggy in the summer. At the same time, the low-lying region's unique geography holds the perfect antidote to hot afternoons: the limestone shelf that forms the peninsula is riddled with underground rivers, accessible at sinkholes called cenotes – a geological phenomenon only found here.

Nature's perfect swimming spots, cenotes are filled with cool fresh water year-round, and they're so plentiful that you're bound to find one nearby when you need a refreshing dip. Some are unremarkable holes in the middle of a farmer's field, while others, like Cenote Azul near Laguna Bacalar, are enormous, deep wells complete with diving platforms and on-site restaurants.

The most visited and photographed cenotes are set in dramatic caverns in and around the old colonial city of Valladolid. Cenote Zací, in the centre of town, occupies a full city block. Half-covered by a shell of rock, the pool exudes a chill that becomes downright cold as you descend the access stairs. Just outside of town, Dzitnup and neighboring Samula are almost completely underground. Shinny down some rickety stairs, and you'll find yourself in cathedral-like spaces, where sound and light bounce off the walls. Both cenotes are beautifully illuminated by the sun, which shines through a hole in the ceiling, forming a glowing spotlight on the turquoise water.

Even more remarkable, however, is that these caverns extend underwater. Strap on a snorkel or scuba gear, and drop below the surface to spy a still world of delicate stalagmites. Exploring these ghostly spaces, it's easy to see why the Maya considered cenotes gateways to the underworld. The liminal sensation is heightened by the clarity of the water, which makes you feel as if you're suspended in air.

need to know

Cenote Zací (daily 8am–6pm; M$10) in Valladolid is in the block formed by calles 34, 36, 37 and 39. **Dzitnup** (daily 7am–6pm; M$20) and **Samula** (daily 8am–5pm; M$20) are 7km west of Valladolid on Hwy-180; wear sturdy shoes and pack an extra layer, as the caves are chilly. There are also numerous cenotes south of **Mérida**, and a few along the Caribbean coast; some of the easiest to visit in this latter area are in a park area called **Hidden Worlds** (@www.hiddenworlds.com.mx).

18 *navigating* the Panama Canal

A cruise through the Panama Canal starts off on a high: at the Pacific entrance a series of mighty locks lifts your boat 26.5m above sea level. From here, you move into the narrow confines of the Gaillard Cut, a deep gash gouged through the hills of the Continental Divide.

As you motor along, your guide will bombard you with statistics and stories: how 160 million cubic metres of earth and rock were excavated by a multinational team of 80,000 labourers to create what was once the largest earth dam and most extensive artificial lake in the world.

Quite apart from its monumental scale, you'll also find that this central artery of global commerce possesses an unexpected beauty. Beyond the cut, your boat enters Lago Gatún, a freshwater lake dotted with jungle-covered islands. The tracts of rainforest here are among the most biodiverse in Central America, and you may spot monkeys and toucans in the treetops, or cayman crocodiles basking on the shore.

In the Canal Zone – an 8km strip on each side of the waterway – you'll see the influence of the US, who maintained it until the beginning of the twenty-first century. Though the military bases have closed, a neat, well-ordered society remains, offering a delicious contrast to the chaotic tropical vitality of the natural environment. Watch, too, for other ships: the sight of a massive container vessel slicing through the lake's placid water, lush forest rising on either side, is truly surreal.

When you reach the other side of the lake, another series of locks brings you back down to sea level. Gliding out into the warm water of the Caribbean, you'll understand why many considered this 80km path between the seas "the greatest liberty ever taken with nature".

need to know
Arrange transits of the canal in Panama City with **Canal and Bay Tours** (℗209 2010 or ℗209 2009, ⓦwww.canalandbaytours. com); book well in advance.

19

wandering the back alleys of
ZACATECAS

*A throng of maybe a
hundred people slowly
meandered through the
streets behind the donkey*

Zacatecas is a sophisticated little city, so I was a bit surprised to see a donkey amble past the café window where I sat, its ears poking through a straw sombrero. Only when I saw that its panniers were full of tequila, and that it was being followed by a dozen hombres in gaudy ponchos blasting away on brass instruments, did things begin to make sense.

I was seeing a *callejóneada* (from *callejón*, or alley). I had heard of these, but had never witnessed one before. I nipped outside, just catching the tail end of the procession as it snaked away down the city's narrow alleys – a throng of maybe a hundred people slowly meandered through the streets behind the donkey. Though we effectively blocked traffic, no one seemed much concerned – *callejóneadas* are a way of life in Zacatecas, and people in the historic centre know to expect a little donkey congestion. Drivers just cranked up their stereos and waited for us to turn down another alley.

Callejóneadas are usually organized to celebrate a special event, like a birthday or a wedding. Someone hires a band and a donkey, then buys enough tequila and small ceramic cups for everyone in the party. Periodically the donkey driver (or one of his enthusiastic assistants) makes the rounds, pouring everyone a shot.

I felt out of place, not having a cup of my own, but I soon made friends and was given one, the tequila purveyor dutifully summoned. Though downing the alcohol in one swift gulp is obligatory, *callejóneadas* aren't about excessive consumption. Rather, they are an excuse to enjoy time with friends (and any strangers who happen along), meander through alleys in the balmy night air, listen to the band and occasionally even dance.

After a while, the band exhausted its repertoire and my companions began to disperse, some going home for a late dinner, others heading straight to the city's bars and clubs, leaving the alleys quiet for another evening.

need to know
Zacatecas (8hr by bus from Mexico City) typically has three or four **callejóneadas** every Friday and Saturday evening (and sometimes Thurs and Sun) around 8pm; just listen, seek and follow. You're usually welcome to join in, though it is courteous to bring your own refreshments.

20
galloping through
Guanacaste

This is not the Costa Rica you may have imagined: one glance at the wide-open spaces, the legions of heat-stunned cattle or the mounted *sabaneros* (cowboys) trotting alongside the Pan-American Highway reveals that Guanacaste has little in common with the rest of the country. Often called "the Texas of Costa Rica", this is ranching territory; the lush, humid rainforest that blankets most of the country is notably absent here, replaced by a swathe of tropical dry forest. It's one of the last significant patches of such land in Central America.

Given the region's livelihood, it's only fitting that the best way to tour Guanacaste is astride a horse. Don't be shy about scrambling into the saddle – many of the working ranches in the province double as hotels, and almost all of them offer horseback tours, giving you a chance to participate in the region's *sabanero* culture. From your perch high above the ground, the strange, silvery beauty of the dry forest appears to much greater advantage – in the dry season, the trees shed their leaves in an effort to conserve water, leaving the landscape eerily bare and melancholy.

You'll be able to spot all kinds of wildlife, from monkeys and pot-bellied iguanas to birds and even the odd boa constrictor (though the horses may not be impressed by this one).

For a different sort of scenery, head to the area around still-active Rincón de la Vieja, where you can ride around bubbling mud pots (*pilas de barro*) and puffing steam vents, all under the shadow of the towering, mist-shrouded volcano.

Some of the region's ranches-cum-hotels even let guests put in a day's work riding out with their hands, provided fence-mending and cattle-herding skills are up to scratch. Regardless of your level of equestrian experience, once you've had a gallop through Guanacaste, you'll never look at sightseeing on foot the same way again.

need to know

There are frequent buses to **Liberia**, the provincial capital, from San José (4hr 30min). Many of the area ranches offer good-value tour packages; of these, **Buena Vista Lodge** (☎661-8158; ⊛www.buenavistacr.com) has the best views.

21

kayaking in the
Sea *of* Cortez

The remote and ruggedly beautiful Baja coastline has become a favourite destination for sea kayakers

Standing on the east coast of Baja California, surveying the peninsula's near-lifeless ochre landscape, it's hard to imagine that a frenzy of nature lies just steps away. But launch a sea kayak into the glistening surf of the Sea of Cortez and you'll find yourself surrounded by rich and varied wildlife – a veritable natural aquarium.

The remote and ruggedly beautiful Baja coastline has become a favourite destination for sea kayakers – and for good reason. The calm waters of the Sea of Cortez make for easy surf launches and smooth paddling. Hundreds of unexplored coves, uninhabited islands and miles of mangrove-lined estuaries play host to sea lions, turtles and nesting birds. Just the shell of your kayak separates you from dolphins, grey whales, coral reefs and over 600 species of fish as you glide through placid lagoons, volcanic caves and natural arches.

It's a good idea to keep your snorkelling gear handy – should you ever tire of the topside scenery, you can make a quick escape to an even more spectacular underwater world. Rookeries of sea lions dot island coasts, and if you approach them slowly, the pups can be especially playful, even mimicking your underwater movements before performing a ballet of their own.

Back on land, as you camp on white-sand beaches and feast on freshly made *ceviche* under the glow of a glorious sunset, you'll have time to enjoy some peace and quiet before pondering your next launch.

need to know
Tour operators in both **Loreto** and **La Paz** offer outfitting, guided expeditions and accommodation, with La Paz providing easier access to the popular **Isla Espíritu Santo** and more rental options for the independent kayaker.

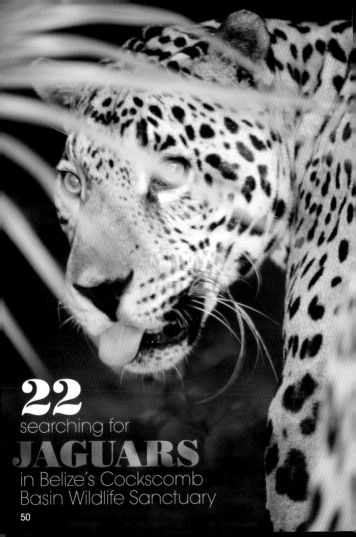

22
searching for
JAGUARS
in Belize's Cockscomb
Basin Wildlife Sanctuary

Looking for tigers? Head to India. Lions or cheetahs? You'll want to be in southern Africa. If it's jaguars you're after, though, few places are more spectacular than the rainforests of Belize.

Here, in the Cockscomb Basin Wildlife Sanctuary, the world's only jaguar reserve, the enormous, elusive wildcats roam freely through one hundred thousand acres of pristine jungle.

According to local guides, sunrise is the best time to glimpse jaguars. Almost every day, eager cat-spotters set out in the small hours from Maya Centre, an indigenous Mopan Maya community and the hub for trips into the reserve. In the half-light, the rainforest teems with wildlife. The trees form a cavernous canopy above your head; in combination with the thick undergrowth, the vegetation can overwhelm – and the atmosphere is intensified by sightings of red-eyed tree frogs, tarantulas, bats and iguanas. Gibnuts – small, rat-like creatures – rustle through the scrub. Keep an eye out for the four other species of wildcats that also call the reserve home, including margay, who favour the canopy, and pumas, who slink through the surrounding mountains. As the forest warms up, 4000 species of flowering plants spring into bloom, and toucans, king vultures and scarlet macaws flit through the trees.

You've come for the jaguars, though, and as the sun climbs in the sky, you still haven't seen one. Let's be honest – you're far more likely to see the eyes of a gibnut shining from the undergrowth than you are the glamorous yet camera-shy felines. It's the hunt that makes Cockscomb so special. You know they're there, and they know you know it – if your wits happen to collide you'll be rewarded with a sight very few people are lucky enough to witness. In the meantime, don't forget to enjoy the natural wonderland around you.

need to know

All buses between Dangriga and Punta Gorda pass **Maya Centre**. Most visitors choose to stay here in a "homestay" with a Maya family; the Saqui family (@nuukcheil@btl.net) and the Chun family (@www.mayacenter.com) offer comfortable accommodation. Or, try the upscale **Kanantik Reef and Jungle Resort** (@www.kanantik.com), 6km south. All of the above arrange trips into the reserve. The park entrance fee is Bz$10.

making peace with

TEQUILA

in Tequila

My first taste of tequila in Tequila was terrible – rough as guts and horribly strong. We were on a tour of one of the area's many distilleries, and the sample had been extracted straight from the production line. My stomach swooped uncomfortably as I looked at the steaming piles of blue agave cactus pulp. Definitely not going back for seconds.

Things began to look up when we entered the distillery's ancient storage sheds: this was where they kept the good stuff as it aged. As yet another round of samples went around, the guide explained the subtleties of the various styles and how best to appreciate them (no, the gringo accompaniments of salt, lime and bare skin are not obligatory). A few sips and my stomach, still nervous about receiving more of the fresh stuff, began to settle down – my conversion was underway.

Light-headed but not entirely sated, we headed back to Guadalajara, where we repaired to La Maestranza, a dimly lit bar festooned with old bullfight memorabilia: half a dozen stuffed bulls heads were arranged above the row of tequila bottles on the top shelf of the bar, as if to drive the point home. Someone ordered us a round of *banderas*, a trio of hefty tumblers that together form the green, white and red of the Mexican flag – the first is half-filled with fresh lime juice, the second with tequila, and the third with *sangrita*, a slightly sweet combination of spicy tomato juice and orange juice. Some chose to savour theirs, conforming to the recommended sequence (the sweetness of the *sangrita* settles the astringency of the tequila), others knocked them back without a second thought, then rapidly ordered another round. And another. All in all, I think that first taste was deceiving.

need to know

Several distilleries around **Tequila** run tours; the most popular is **José Cuervo** (Wwww.cuervo. com). The basic tour (M$75) runs 1hr and includes a free sample; for an extra M$32 you learn the full tasting etiquette and the difference between styles, and receive a free margarita. Buses run to Tequila regularly from Guadalajara (1 hr 45min). **La Maestranza** is at Maestranza 179, in Guadalajara.

53

climbing

El Castillo

at Chichén Itzá

*Clambering up the impossibly steep face
of the central pyramid of Chichén Itzá,
nicknamed "the castle" by the Spaniards,
you can't help but count your steps.
And that's exactly what the ancient
Maya wanted you to do.*

By the time you reach the platform at the top (25m above the grassy lawn at the base), you should have counted to 91. After you've caught your breath and got your vertigo under control, do a little math: 91 steps up each of the four sides of the structure totals 364. Add the step you're standing on, and you get, not coincidentally, the number of days in a year.

The Maya were obsessed with the passage of time. Their complex calendar system completed a full cycle every 52 years, and with that came certain rituals. The seemingly solid pyramid you're standing on encases a second, smaller one. According to the glyphs on the buildings, the *castillo* was built 52 years after its miniature core.

The pyramid is dedicated to Kukulcán, the feathered serpent who headed the Maya pantheon. His gaping mouth adorns either side of the main set of stairs, but his full image emerges only at the spring and fall equinoxes, when the sun creates a long, snaking shadow up the staircase.

But given how little archeologists have been able to discern about Maya culture after centuries of study, how true is this interpretation of the monument? What seem like resonant facts to us – the number of steps, the shadow – may have meant next to nothing to the Maya, and the real object of their fascination could still lie well beyond our reach.

At the base of El Castillo, the scene is one of modern tourist mayhem, with guides spinning tales about the people who once inhabited the place. From your perch far above the fray, however, you get the feeling that many of the Maya's secrets are still locked in these stones.

need to know
Chichén Itzá (daily 8am–5pm; M$88) is about four hours from Cancún. Guided tours are available for about M$300. Try to get there before 10am, when the tour buses arrive. Accommodation is available in the adjacent village of Pisté or the colonial city of Valladolid.

honouring the dead in
JANITZIO

Mexicans believe that the thin veil between the land of the living and the world of the spirits is at its most permeable on the night of November 1, as All Saints' Day slips silently into All Souls' Day. This is the one time each year, it is said, when the dead can visit the relatives they have left behind. Mexicans all over the country aim to make them feel welcome when they do, though nowhere are the preparations as elaborate as

on the island of Janitzio in Lake Pátzcuaro.

Market stalls laden with papier-mâché skeletons and sugar skulls appear weeks in advance; the decorations and sweets go on shrines set up in people's homes. Dedicated to the departed, the shrines come complete with a photo of the deceased and an array of their favourite treats – perhaps some cigarettes, a few tamales and, of course, preferred brands of tequila and beer.

When the big day comes, you don't want to arrive too early at the cemetery – it isn't until around 11pm, as the witching hour approaches, that the island's indigenous Purhépecha people start filtering into the graveyard. They come equipped with candles, incense and wooden frames draped in a riot of puffy orange marigolds. Pretty soon the entire site is aglow with candles, the abundantly adorned graves slightly eerie in the flickering light. So begins the all-night vigil: some observers doze silently, others reminisce with friends seated at nearby graves. It is a solemn, though by no means sombre, occasion. Indeed, unlike most cultures, Mexicans live with death and celebrate it.

By early morning the cemetery is peaceful, and in the pre-dawn chill, as sleep threatens to overtake you, it is easier to see how the dead could be tempted back for a brief visit, and why people return year after year to commune with the departed.

need to know

The town of Pátzcuaro, on the shores of Lake Pátzcuaro, is the main staging point for boat trips to **Janitzio** (M$30 return); boats run throughout the night. Accommodation in **Pátzcuaro** for the Day of the Dead should be booked at least six months in advance.

25

Ultimate
experiences
Mexico &
Central America
miscellany

Language

Spanish is the official language of Mexico and the countries of Central America, with the sole exception of Belize, where people speak a type of patois – English with a lilting accent, simplified grammar and phonetic spelling. The Amerindians of Mexico and Guatemala also have their own dialects. Mexican Spanish is very distinct, with drawn-out nasal cadences and lots of expression. Guatemalans tend to speak very slowly and clearly. Hondurans and El Salvadorans have strong regional accents, while Nicaraguans are known for the variety and richness of their slang. Panamanians speak a kind of Caribbean Spanish, similar to Cubans or Puerto Ricans.

"Love is blind. But not the neighbours."

Mexican proverb

 # Ethnicities

Most Mexicans and Central Americans are of Spanish, West African or Amerindian descent. Mixed-race people (Spanish and Amerindian) are called mestizo and form the majority of the region's population. Thirty percent of Mexicans are Amerindian and identified as indigenous peoples (Maya, Mixtec, Zapotec, Toltec and Purépecha among them), and almost half of Guatemalans are pure-blooded Maya – K'iche, Kaqchikel, Mam and Q'eqchi. Belize has a strong Creole culture, created by descendants of black slaves and British colonists, and more akin to that of the Caribbean than the rest of the region. Smaller Creole communities are also evident on the Caribbean coasts of Guatemala, Honduras, Nicaragua, Costa Rica and Panama.

Ecotourism

Ecotourism was practically invented in Central America. **Costa Rica** has the most organized network of national parks and reserves in the region; 27 percent of the country's territory is now protected. The densely forested interior of **Belize** is largely undamaged, and boasts Central America's highest waterfall, Thousand-Foot Falls, and the world's only jaguar reserve, Cockscomb Basin Wildlife Sanctuary. **Panama's** great biodiversity is showcased in two enormous wildlife havens, Parque Nacional Darién, where over five hundred species of birds have been spotted, and Parque Internacional La Amistad, which encompasses nine biological life zones, or vegetative communities.

▶▶ Five great ecolodges

The Lodge at Chaa Creek, Belize. Thatched cottages in gorgeous grounds high above the Macal River, in the foothills of the Maya Mountains.

Caves Branch Jungle Lodge, Belize. Accommodation for every budget on the banks of the Caves Branch River; excellent guided tours of area caves containing Classic-period Maya artefacts.

Corcovado Tent Camp, Costa Rica. Self-contained "tent camps" elevated on short stilts right on the beach near Carate.

Reserva Selva Bananito, Costa Rica. Truly ecoconscious accommodation: cottages are built from wood abandoned by loggers, and they rely on solar power.

Canopy Tower, Panama. A former US radar station in Parque Nacional Soberaniá, the rooms are in a refitted geodesic dome.

4 Zócalo

The centre of every Mexican town, big or small, is its *zócalo* (main square). Evenings see food vendors wheeling their carts into the streets, balloon-sellers touting their multi-coloured wares, café tables filled with patrons and roving musicians breaking into their repertoires. Three of the most distinctive *zócalos* in Mexico are in Mexico City, Oaxaca and Veracruz.

5 Literature

▶▶ Five books by Mexican and Central American authors

One Day of Life by Manlio Argueta. A day in the life of one fictional El Salvadoran family caught up in the country's civil war.

Men of Maize by Miguel Angel Asturias. Experimental novel dealing with the desecration of indigenous Maya culture in Guatemala.

The Country Under My Skin by Gioconda Belli. Nicaraguan poet's memoir of her evolution from traditional upper-class wife to Sandinista revolutionary and government minister.

The Death of Artemio Cruz by Carlos Fuentes. A wealthy, dying businessman reflects on his life, focusing on the Mexican Revolution and the post-war years.

Labyrinth of Solitude by Octavio Paz. Originally published in 1950, poet Paz's influential study of Mexican character and thought.

▶▶ Five books about Mexico and Central America

A Visit to Don Octavio by Sybille Bedford. Colourful and amusing account of a 1952 trip to Mexico by two intrepid English women.

Tekkin' A Waalk by Peter Ford. Ford's story of his trip along the Caribbean coast of Central America; he encounters Miskito Indians, Garífuna and pirate lore along the way.

The Soccer War by Rysard Kapuscinski. Account by Polish journalist of the 100-hour war between El Salvador and Honduras in 1969.

The Tailor of Panama by John le Carré. Spy thriller stuffed with fascinating insight into Panamanian society.

The Mosquito Coast by Paul Theroux. Fast-paced novel about an idealist who moves his family to the untamed jungles of Honduras.

"There's more time than life."
Nicaraguan proverb

Civil war

Mexico suffered two notable uprisings in the twentieth century: the **Mexican Revolution** (1910–17), waged by such colourful characters as Pancho Villa and Emiliano Zapata; and the **formation of the EZLN** (Ejercito Zapatista de Liberacion Nacional, commonly known as the **Zapatistas**) in the impoverished state of Chiapas in 1983. A series of skirmishes to protest the inception of NAFTA in January 1994 announced this group's presence to the international scene. Since then, the Zapatistas have been involved in several peaceful campaigns to reform the government and constitution.

Nicaragua, El Salvador and Guatemala were ravaged by civil war during the late twentieth century, as liberals and indigenous peoples seeking land reform and democracy stood against brutal military governments supported by conservative landowners and the American CIA (which sought to keep communism out of the region). Hundreds of thousands of civilians died, were tortured or simply "disappeared" in the conflicts. Peace accords were signed in the 1990s, and all three countries now exist as fragile, though promising, democracies.

7 Mañana

Time is a fairly elastic concept in Mexico and Central America. "*Ahorita*" is a well-used phrase meaning "right now", though things rarely actually happen that way. Local buses leave when they're full or the driver has finished his lunch, and appointments often begin several hours after their scheduled start times. Meals – except at busy lunchtimes – often take an hour to arrive at the table. All in all, you'll enjoy your trip far more if you go with the flow and just say "*mañana, mañana*" ("tomorrow, tomorrow") along with the rest of them.

8 Coral reefs

The world's second largest coral reef, the Mesoamerican Barrier Reef, lies off the Caribbean coast of Mexico, Belize, Guatemala and Honduras, making the region a magnificent aquatic playground. Hot spots for scuba diving and snorkelling, the two most popular pursuits, include the Mexican island of **Cozumel**, Belize's cayes (tiny islands; home to three atolls and the Blue Hole, a collapsed cave made famous by Jacques Cousteau) and the **Bay Islands** of Honduras.

9 Birds

There are over a thousand species of birds in Mexico and Central America. The most sought-after by birders are the quetzal, with its shimmering green and red feathers; the scarlet macaw (*lapa*); and the toucan. Some places to look include:

Quetzal Cloudforests of Guatemala, Nicaragua and Costa Rica

Scarlet macaws Parque Nacional Corcovado, Costa Rica, and Parque Nacional Darién, Panama

Toucans Along the Pacific coast; especially in Parque Nacional Soberanía, Panama

10 The Maya

One of the western hemisphere's most sophisticated **pre-Columbian civilizations**, the Maya flourished in Mexico and northern Central America between 300 and 900 AD. An intricate calendar based on the solar year, an advanced form of hieroglyphics and enormous temples are just a few elements of the Maya legacy. Several million pure-blooded Maya, particularly in southern Mexico and the western highlands of Guatemala, live according to ancient custom: traditional costume is still worn in many areas (especially by women), a number of indigenous languages are still spoken and some remote tribes even observe the 260-day Tzolkin calendar.

11 Lakes and rivers

Central America is laced with lakes (several of them vast), rivers and canals. The longest rivers flow into the Caribbean Sea, while many smaller waterways drain into the Pacific Ocean. Travelling by boat in these areas is a fascinating, though uncomfortable, experience (be prepared to get wet).

▶▶ Longest rivers of Central America

COUNTRY	NAME OF RIVER	LENGTH
Honduras	Coco	800km
Nicaragua	Grande	430km
Guatemala	Motagua	400km
El Salvador	Lempa	320km
Belize	Belize	290km
Costa Rica	Grande de Teraba	198km
Panama	Tuira	170km

12 Hammocks

Long used (think pre-Columbus) by Amerindians, hammocks are still the main form of bedding for the region's indigenous peoples. Budget hotels often have hammock space available for a few dollars a night, and anyone attempting a long boat trip will need a hammock – cabins on boats rarely exist. One of the best places to buy a colourful string hammock in the region is Mérida, in Mexico's Yucatán Peninsula.

13 Don't drink the water

Delicious non-alcoholic drinks include freshly made fruit juices (*jugos* and *licuados*), flavoured waters (*aguas frescas* – the most popular are *jamaica*, made from hibiscus flowers, and *tamarindo*) and *horchata* (milk made from rice and almonds, served chilled). Beer, usually lager-style *cerveza clara*, is available everywhere. Spirits include Mexican tequila and less well-known *mescal* (made from maguey cactus and like a rough, woody tequila), and in Central America, *aguardiente* (aniseed-flavoured and translucent).

▶▶ Five drinks to try

Seaweed, Belize. A blend of seaweed, milk, cinnamon, sugar and cream; strangely delicious.

Guifiti, Honduras. A distilled moonshine flavoured with cloves and tasting a bit like toothache medication, available in the north coast Garífuna villages.

Pitahaya juice, Nicaragua. Made from the fruit of a cactus, it's a virulent purple in color – it'll probably stain your tongue.

Guaro, Costa Rica. An indigenous sugarcane-based spirit; Cacique is the most popular brand.

Hot chocolate, Mexico. Not the drink of your childhood – here it's spicy and semi-bitter, often flavoured with chilli powder.

14 Rice and beans

Food in Central America is fairly basic – the standard diet is rice and beans accompanied by chunks of meat, fried fish or eggs – though most every country has at least one specialty dish. Chilli sauce is ubiquitous and spices up the otherwise bland fare. Mexican food is more sophisticated, with complicated *moles* (sauces), stews and lime-flavoured seafood cocktails.

▶▶ Five foods to try

Chiles en nogada, Mexico. Stuffed green peppers covered in a white sauce (walnuts and either cream cheese or sour cream) and pomegranate.

Pupusas, El Salvador. Small tortillas filled with cheese, beans and pork crackling, and served piping hot with tomato juice, hot sauce and *curtido* (pickled cabbage, beetroot and carrots).

Sancocho, Panama. A hearty chicken soup with yucca, plantains and other root vegetables and flavoured with coriander.

Anafre, Honduras. A fondue-like dish of cheese, beans or meat, or some combination of all three.

Ron don, Nicaragua. "To cook", in local parlance – a stew of yucca, chayote and other vegetables, and some kind of meat; it's simmered for at least a day and traditionally eaten at weekends.

15 Festivals

Practically every community in Mexico and Central America has an annual fiesta, a heady mix of parades, costumes, arcane customs, music and dancing, all topped off with fireworks and traditional food. Many fiestas are tied to saints' days, but some are connected to events from pre-Columbian history. The most colourful local festivals take place in Mexico's indigenous communities and Guatemala's western highlands, while the largest celebrated in the whole region are Semana Santa (Holy Week) and the Day of the Dead (November 1).

▶▶ Five great festivals

Fiesta de la Virgen de la Candelaria, San Blas, Mexico (Feb 1–3). The patron saint of the fishing community is taken out in a boat to bless the sea.

Baron Bliss Day, Belize (March 9). Celebration in honour of one of the country's greatest benefactors; there's a regatta in Belize City and smaller boat races across the country.

Fiesta de Maíz, Danlí, Honduras (last weekend in Aug). The town celebrates the corn harvest with parades, corn recipes and an all-night street party.

Fiesta of the Black Christ, Portobelo, Panama (Oct 21). In a wild and chaotic celebration of faith, thousands of devotees descend on the town to pay homage to its patron saint.

Todos Santos, Cuchumatán, Guatemala (Oct 29–Nov 1). The village celebrates for three days around the Day of the Dead with horse races, marimba bands and public displays of drunkenness.

16 Climate

There are two distinct seasons: wet (or rainy), which lasts from May to October and is often called *invierno* (winter), and dry, which runs from November to April and is known as *verano* (summer). Temperature is dictated more by altitude than latitude. For example, Acapulco and San Cristóbal are both at sixteen degrees latitude. In December in Acapulco, which is at sea level, average temperature is 24°C; in San Cristóbal, at 2000m, it's 12°C.

17 Cocks and bulls

Cockfighting is a popular backwoods sport in Mexico (where it is legal and official arenas – *plazas de gallos* – exist). Birds are specially trained for months, substantial bets are laid and fights go on until one of two cocks is killed by the other (metal spurs are attached to their legs). Bullfighting is also still popular in Mexico; the world's largest bullfighting ring, Plaza México, is in Mexico City. Neither of these are spectator sports for the squeamish.

"It's better to be a living chicken than a dead cockerel".

Mexican proverb

18 Rum

Rum (*ron*) is the celebratory drink of choice in most of Central America. Each country has its own distilleries, and the local brew can usually be bought for a few dollars. The best rum comes from Guatemala and Nicaragua; both countries have produced award-winning aged spirits – *Zacapa Centenario* and *Flor de Caña Centenario* respectively. It's virtually impossible to find Central American rum outside the region, making a bottle of the good stuff (US$10–25) an excellent souvenir.

19 Political murals

Wall paintings were made popular shortly after the Mexican Revolution by three artists: Diego Rivera, David Siqueiros and José Clemente Orozco. Their enormous, vibrant murals can still be seen today in government buildings and town halls all over the country. In Central America, the civil wars of the 1970s and 80s spawned a number of naïve paintings depicting revolutionaries and their tormenters. To this day, official political campaigns are hand-painted on the sides of buildings, walls and even telegraph poles throughout the region.

▶▶ Five memorable murals

The People and Its Leaders, José Clemente Orozco. Government Palace, Guadalajara

Sandino mural, Mausoleo Héroes y Mártires. Léon, Nicaragua

History of Mexico, Diego Rivera. National Palace, Mexico City

March of Humanity, David Alfaro Siqueiros. Hotel de Mexico, Mexico City

The Hospicio Cabañas frescoes, José Clemente Orozco. Guadalajara

20 Tubular heaven

The Pacific coast of Mexico and Central America has a long-established reputation among surfers for consistent waves and uncrowded waters. Top spots in Mexico include most of the Baja Peninsula, particularly Punta el Conejo and Todos Santos; Puerto Escondido, on the Oaxaca coast; and around Lázaro Cárdenas in Michoacan. There are very good point breaks in El Salvador, with several surfing beaches along the coast west of La Libertad. San Juan del Sur in Nicaragua has a large expat surfing community. Costa Rica actually has breaks on its Caribbean coast – the *salsa brava* at Puerto Viejo is the country's biggest wave.

21 Volcanoes

Mexico and Central America are home to almost one hundred volcanoes (most are found in Mexico, Costa Rica, El Salvador, Guatemala and Nicaragua) – the region is part of the "ring of fire", a zone of frequent volcanic eruptions and earthquakes that encircles the Pacific Basin. A handful of these volcanoes are still considered active, and it's possible to see spectacular light shows of molten lava at Arenal in Costa Rica and Picaya in Guatemala. Most, however, have long been dormant, leaving their slopes open to hikers.

▶▶ Top five volcanoes to climb

Nevado de Colima, Mexico (4335m)
Volcán de Santa María, Guatemala (3372m)
Volcán de Santa Ana, El Salvador (2365m)
Volcán Maderas, Nicaragua (1395m)
Volcán Barú, Panama (3475m)

22 Garífuna

The Garífuna are descendents of black slaves who were shipwrecked en route from Nigeria to America and integrated with the Caribs of St Vincent. Later chased by the Spanish to the Bay Islands of Honduras and then to the mainland, they now live along the coasts of Honduras, Belize and Guatemala and number less than 200,000. Many aspects of Garífuna culture – including their language (*igñeri*), mesmeric drum-based music (*punta*) and spirit worship – stem from their West African heritage. **Garífuna Settlement Day** (Nov 19) is one of the best opportunities for visitors to observe Garífuna traditions, especially in the Belizean towns of Dangriga and Hopkins.

Music

Ranchera, Mexico's version of country and western (complete with wailing tones and lyrics of loss, longing and patriotism), is the country's most popular form of music. Though the name is derived from *rancho*, which means farm, *ranchera* originated from the nostalgia felt by town dwellers for their homelands in post-revolution Mexico. These days, *ranchera* has been adapted by **norteño** (Tex-Mex) musicians to reflect contemporary social issues, especially illegal immigration and drug running. The most successful *norteño* band is Grammy-winning Los Tigres del Norte.

▶▶ Five great ranchera/norteño albums

Lola la Grande (2003)   Lola Beltrán

El Idolo de Mexico (1994)   Vicente Fernandez

La Sota de Copas (2003)   José Alfredo Jiménez

La Historia de Javier Solis (1992)   Javier Solis

Jefe de Jefes (1997)   Los Tigres del Norte

24 Tortillas

Tortillas are thin circular pancakes made from corn and usually served warm, in a cloth-wrapped pile. They've been a staple in Mexico and Central America since pre-Columbian times. You can see them being made in the traditional manner in rural areas of Mexico, Guatemala and El Salvador – maize is ground into a paste with a stone *metate* (small concave table), then patted by hand into perfect circles and toasted over an open fire.

25 Mexico in the movies

Mexico has a thriving film industry, one of the world's oldest: by 1906, the popularity of imported silent movies was so great that there were sixteen cinemas in Mexico City. The home-grown film business saw its golden age during the 1940s, with a huge output (70 films in 1943 alone) and stars such as Cantiflas (the Mexican Charlie Chaplin) and Dolores del Rio. In the 1950s and 60s the country became known for its cult horror flicks, many of which are essential viewing for film buffs; recent dramas like *Amores perros* and *Y tu mama también* have once again brought Mexico to the forefront of the international film scene.

▶▶ Five classic Mexican horror flicks

El Hombre sin rostro (The Man Without a Face), dir. Juan Bustillo Oro, 1950.

El Vampiro (The Vampire), dir. Fernando Méndez, 1957.

El Espejo de la bruja (The Witch's Mirror), dir. Chano Urueta 1962.

El Santo contras las mujeres vampiro (Santo Against the Female Vampires), dir. Alfonso Corona Blake, 1962.

La Horripilante bestia humana (Night of the Bloody Apes), dir. René Cardona, 1969.

25 Ultimate experiences
Mexico & Central America
Small print

ROUGH GUIDES – don't just travel

We hope you've been inspired by the experiences in this book. To us, they sum up what makes Mexico and Central America such an extraordinary and stimulating place to travel. There are 24 other books in the 25 Ultimate Experiences series, each conceived to whet your appetite for travel and for everything the world has to offer. As well as covering the globe, the 25s series also includes books on **Journeys, World Food, Adventure Travel, Places to Stay, Ethical Travel, Wildlife Adventures** and **Wonders of the World.**

When you start planning your trip, Rough Guides' new-look guides, maps and phrasebooks are the ultimate companions. For 25 years we've been refining what makes a good guidebook and we now include more colour photos and more information – on average 50% more pages – than any of our competitors. Just look for the sky-blue spines.

Rough Guides don't just travel – we also believe in getting the most out of life without a passport. Since the publication of the bestselling Rough Guides to **The Internet** and **World Music**, we've brought out a wide range of lively and authoritative guides on everything from **Climate Change** to **Hip-Hop**, from **MySpace** to **Film Noir** and from **The Brain** to **The Rolling Stones.**

Publishing information

Rough Guide 25 Ultimate experiences Mexico & Central America Published May 2007 by Rough Guides Ltd, 80 Strand, London WC2R 0RL

345 Hudson St, 4th Floor, New York, NY 10014, USA

14 Local Shopping Centre, Panchsheel Park, New Delhi 110017, India

Distributed by the Penguin Group

Penguin Books Ltd,
80 Strand, London WC2R 0RL

Penguin Group (USA)
375 Hudson Street, NY 10014, USA

Penguin Group (Australia)
250 Camberwell Road, Camberwell, Victoria 3124, Australia

Penguin Books Canada Ltd.
10 Alcorn Avenue, Toronto, Ontario, Canada M4V 1E4

Penguin Group (NZ)
67 Apollo Drive, Mairangi Bay, Auckland 1310, New Zealand

Printed in China
© Rough Guides 2007

80pp
A catalogue record for this book is available from the British Library
ISBN: 978-1-84353-823-3

Rough Guide credits

Editor: Ella Steim
Design & picture research: Cosima Dinkel
Cartography: Katie Lloyd-Jones, Maxine Repath

Cover design: Diana Jarvis, Chloë Roberts
Production: Aimee Hampson, Katherine Owers
Proofreader: Amy Hegarty

The authors

Polly Rodger Brown (Experiences 1, 5, 10, 14, 15, Miscellany) is co-author of the *Rough Guide First-Time Latin America*.

Jean McNeil (Experiences 2, 20) writes the *Rough Guide to Costa Rica*.

Caroline Lascom (Experiences 3, 12) contributes to the *Rough Guide to Mexico*.

Richard Arghiris (Experience 4) contributes to the *Rough Guide to Mexico*.

Jason Clampet (Experience 6) is author of the *Rough Guide to Baja California*.

Iain Stewart (Experiences 7, 11, 16) writes the *Rough Guide to Guatemala*.

Zora O'Neill (Experiences 8, 13, 17, 24) writes Rough Guides to the Yucatán and Cancún and Cozumel, and is an author of the Rough Guide to Mexico.

James Read (Experiences 9, 18) is co-author of the *Rough Guide First-Time Latin America*.

Paul Whitfield (Experiences 19, 23, 25) is an author of the *Rough Guide to Mexico*.

Gregory Witt (Experience 21) leads adventure-travel trips all over the world.

Rob Coates (Experience 22) contributes to the *Rough Guide to Belize*.

Picture credits

Cover Day of the Dead offering in the Dolores Olmedo Patiño Museum of Fine Art © Danita Delimont/Alamy
8–9 Mariachi band © Bruce Herman/Getty
10–11 Leatherback turtle © Britt Dyer/South American Pictures
12–13 Woman embroidering © Danny Lehman/Corbis; Purification ritual, San Juan de Chamula © Robert van der Hilst/Corbis
14–15 Copper Canyon National Park © Michel Tcherevkoff/Getty
16–17 Man surfing at the Pacific Coast © Mark Lewis/Alamy
18–19 Taco stand © Kim Karpeles/Alamy; Fish taco © Thomas Shjarback/Alamy
20–21 View from Temple IV, Tikal © James Strachan/Getty
22–23 Soft coral, Palancar Reef © Sami Sarkis/Alamy
24–25 Kuna woman © Robert Harding Picture Library Ltd/Alamy; Traditional Kuna boat © Robert Harding Picture Library Ltd/Alamy
26–27 Decorative boats © Danita Delimont/Alamy
28–29 Whale shark and diver © Mike Kelly/Getty
30–31 Flower vendor © Lindsay Hebberd/Corbis; Produce stand © Bob Krist/Corbis; Handicrafts © Bruce Herman/Getty
32–33 Bonampak battle scene, Museo Nacional de Antropología © Bridgeman Art Library; Temples at Bonampak © Fabienne Fossez/Alamy
34–35 El Castillo on the Río San Juan © Fabienne Fossez/Alamy; Howler monkeys ©

Juniors Bildarchiv/Alamy; Scarlet macaw © britishcolumbiaphotos.com/Alamy
36–37 Mole Poblano © Anthony Blake Photo Library; Harvested chillis © Catherine Karnow/Corbis; Hanging chillis © Catherine Karnow/Corbis
38–39 Easter celebration, Antigua © Robert Francis/South American Pictures; Carpet of coloured sawdust, Antigua © Robert Francis/South American Pictures; Boy and man dressed as Roman soldiers © Robert Francis/South American Pictures
40–41 Swimming in a cenote © Macduff Everton/Getty
42–43 Ships in the Panama Canal © Danny Lehman/Corbis
44–45 Zacatecas at night © Mitch Diamond/Alamy; Mariachi band © Peter M. Wilson/Alamy
46–47 Volcán Rincón de la Vieja © RH Productions/Robert Harding; Horses © RH Productions/Robert Harding; Horses grazing © RH Productions/Robert Harding
48–49 Sea kayaking © DanitaDelimont.com/Alamy
50–51 Jaguar © Peter Lilja/Getty
52–53 Agave plant © Lisa Romerein/Getty; Tequila and lime © Mark Lewis/Getty; Mexicans at bar in Cholula © Mel Wineburger/Alamy
54–55 Stone snake head © Gordon Gahan, National Geographic/Getty
56–57 Day of the Dead on Janitzio Island © Tom Owen Edmunds/Getty; Candy skulls © Tom Owen Edmunds/Getty; Mask for Day of the Dead © Brian Stablyck/Getty

Over 70 reference books and hundreds of travel
guides, maps & phrasebooks that cover the world.